Shouldering

poems by

Julia Leverone

Finishing Line Press
Georgetown, Kentucky

Shouldering

Copyright © 2016 by Julia Leverone
ISBN 978-1-944899-49-3 First Edition
All rights reserved under International and Pan-American Copyright Conventions.
No part of this book may be reproduced in any manner whatsoever without written permission from the publisher, except in the case of brief quotations embodied in critical articles and reviews.

ACKNOWLEDGMENTS

I am thankful to the editors at the following magazines who have published individual poems appearing in this chapbook:

"Reckon," *B O D Y*
"Dents," *Cimarron Review*
"Haze," "Residence," and "Confines," *Crab Orchard Review*
"Quarry Pile," *Leveler*
"Driving to Rose Haven," *Sugar House Review*

Note: The italicized line in "On Mothering" is from Louise Glück's title poem of the book *The Wild Iris*.

Publisher: Leah Maines

Editor: Christen Kincaid

Cover Art: Julia Leverone

Author Photo: Timothy Bergman

Cover Design: Elizabeth Maines

Printed in the USA on acid-free paper.
Order online: www.finishinglinepress.com
also available on amazon.com

Author inquiries and mail orders:
Finishing Line Press
P. O. Box 1626
Georgetown, Kentucky 40324
U. S. A.

Table of Contents

Dents 1

Driving to Rose Haven 2

Call 3

Weir 4

Haze 5

Residence 6

Run 7

Quarry Pile 8

Clear 9

Triumph 10

Prelude 11

Campground 12

Caribou 13

Correction 14

On Mothering 15

Morning 16

Confines 17

The Orchard 18

Reckon 19

Beam 20

*Voy—río negro—en cruces, en ángulos, en yo no sé qué
retorcimientos de agonía, hacia ti, mar mío, mar ensoñado,
en la punta quimérica y fatal de nuestra distancia.*

I run—black river—in crosses, in angles, in I don't know what
twistings of agony, toward you, my sea, dreamed sea,
to the elusive and final joining of our distances.

—Dulce María Loynaz, "Agua ciega"

Dents

The alley light behind our new lot has a different hue than the others, other than the market's, buzzing blue-green from the route. Multicolored stars hang on the tree. I forget whether we can actually see the school's lit field from here, lit high with stadium lights, and mistake them for a semi lined with rows of yellow bulbs. Blank side: the field's glow. It starts to move. Planes cross above. One reaches with its brass note as from pursed lips, through cupped hands, and coats the moment: which is a brand of love. The neighbor tries her lighter. Something shudders. The tree in our yard is unbudded and grows above things hung with seed. It is forced to look on jealously. I can't quite hear my neighbor speaking—planes, cars, hums, wind through the yard—so her s's lift into a pattern I mistake, for seconds, for her quick drags as if now more upset or nervous, or wakened, aware.

Driving to Rose Haven

These red-painted barns have no age.
Where they are red, they are red
on vertical boards seen through
to the other side—that light
more vivid in slit shapes—
and weathered, weathered down
to gray dead wood beneath.
This is Sansbury Road.
I know it from my childhood.

There are sheep over on the next farm,
the only sign of yield
on the slope that leads
right up to the lip of pavement.
There, a black vulture waits
for something inland, one eye watching.
I am the interference I have made
myself to be. I am on my way
to places that have stayed without me.

Now, the facile coastal rural trend
breaks and sidles up with bay—
blue and tall behind the trees
and down the hill—like how one wave
jarred from the smack of a seawall
reverberates back out, meets another
from the open water, strong and paced,
and they raise each other high
and draw their weight away.

Call

Vigil-late, our noises ceased, we carry outside
our heat into pooled moon-spots strong-set
through the pines, the same that rile in day
like in a robust port how sun echoes off the crests,
off tilted hulls, off glass and metal hardware—
and are now completely still. This white slanting
bright enough for travel. We travel lightly, staying
close, over grounds strange like a stage set
so counter to the real are we, to bodies'
clocks, to night and nature, to habit. I for one
have changed so much to be here.
Like what has lifted up to glide, the wind leaving
overnight. Then the loons' call in the morning.

Weir

A black-haired girl stood fixed on me as I came through,
her brothers around the fire lighting sticks, crowding the pit.

Nearby was the smell of strain, machinery smoke tangy,
the sand's dark ash cut into tracks and mud—motorhomes and gear

dug in, great contained territories behind the dunes. All led
to a mouth, all got swallowed. Kasilof into inlet, Alaskan Gulf,

Pacific tide my timing saw roll out—and the sweet reds, brightest,
running with it, and the men and their nets aligned. So easy to float

in close, summer, to the others wearing old waders in off-colors,
sweatshirts. Just apart, leaning aluminum javelins on their necks—

all feeling, waiting to begin the rush and flux between the beach,
to draw the crackling line like fire working in the shallows,

belly flashing over fin, water renouncing the silt's chalk veil.
Those nets that could take their bearers whole.

Haze

It wasn't heavy pollen from the trees
in the air today—it was their burning,
blown wild smoke from Quebec
and over New Hampshire, descended
around us. The wind we heard would turn
out to sea didn't, fueling, escalating.

I've seen wind on lakes touch down
to give the surface grained
brush strokes, mesmerizing in that
they seemed to move and not move—
then in a second pivot, strike off
and touch the other side the way fire
takes air in, with littered spikes,
erratically, chancing on what's newer
in wakes, waiting for the give.

Residence
> *Iguazu Falls, Argentina*

The Great Dusky Swift
has a coloring soft like attic boxes

crumbling in dust and silted piles,
above a house that's captained by the new

occupant's two large dogs—the magnolia
still there but looking ragged.

The bird packs dark knives for wings,
unknowingly or knowingly. It sleeps

on updrafts in the misted dropoff—
sails and falls—free to cut

from that thunderous, that incessant place
but remains. We go once, see

what's to see, throw coins or watch in quiet,
dark flecks against the water's thrust.

Run

I am at ease. I settle like lake at sundown of a day of staggered sails, of tentative-swift skies, cut propulsions. Dragonflies. I am at ease rowing out on this chipped dinghy, getting my legs into it,

the brace, the pull, the glide, so that the boat is my body and I am running without the stays that dug and tore my docile flesh for hesitating. I cannot believe disturbances—of my doing—remain.

The surface kicking, giddy about itself. I have been wasted. I am at ease. I have been dwelling like the hundred mayflies damned on the cement, unflinching, hailing the dock lights, the softness of the lights, suspended there, not fearing, shoulders opening to sky.

Quarry Pile

Before my brother was born: a rockfall
we foraged. I remember onliness, quiet business,

the cascading at once imminent and stilled,
a bed cleared down a hillside. The sick seep

of milky weed, of summer and dust. Beryl,
quartz? We climbed apart to browse, brooding,

to cover maximum ground. I remember the scrape
and sound of grit in plastic pails, how the turning

of the littered specimens, mostly granite,
caught my hands in little cuts; the weight
numbed them hot.

                    So, my hands left me. This was
a temporary and natural biological defense.

I touched plants to ease them: they came back
stung. For every black leaping moth there must

have been garnet, for ground wasps amethyst—
but these resisted me. Apatite, tourmaline.

Clear

How training works: fifty turns in practice a day, at least. He carves the memory of anchoring at mid-cheek—carves the shoulder position. The sure shot. The ease. His surprise when the arrow passes straight through, and, painted, into a tree. The conundrum of how. Then, the conundrum of a blood trail. Strung red cloud pattern, clotting on the leaves. He wonders when things start to die. Dying at leaving —dying apart? Like loosening hair or cleaning sand into a clear stream.

Triumph

We still tried to see it after we didn't think we could
anymore, our miniature raft of reeds and sea grass, hand-tied

with a crab claw mounted on the mast, joint free to swing.
There was a keel, too, and arm supports off either side,

and we named it, tested it before release: then our idle
project, triumphant, caught the current of the escaping

tide, rode past the beach dunes lined with fishing poles
in sawed-off PVC spikes, the hooks that weren't tugging,

the weights that were gradually drawing up to the sand
with each wash of wave pushing, and underneath, eroding
soft barrier into sea.

Prelude

The first boy swatted at the brush
with a stick, looking for something good to hit
on the path that traversed the harbor island,
making his way to one of its ends. The second

was the same age, or just older, a brother
driving a plastic wheelbarrow
with haste in the same direction.
Marked haste, for the heat—he was taking

something somewhere in a tub of water
in that wheelbarrow, down that path,
past where the first boy was, past the two of us
picking blackberries, you wandering some,

me almost singing to the bushes.
We were like small deer, all stopping to watch.
We all wanted the water despite the salt.
We each had our reasons, and agreed,

nothing good to do but give the thing
half a chance, whatever it was sloshing
at each bump, headed for the end

with the tidal pools, clear pools
in which even we could see everything.
Where the hordes of gulls had easy pickings.

They trained their sight and dove, grasping on,
gliding up, tilted for balance and sifted again
through their vision for a large, flat rock.

Campground

In that capture of mythic wilderness,
off the trail and glacial stream, that blue reach:
a patch of cathedral spires, the Columbine, floral spurs red
and nodding towards the earth I thought were rarities.
I was a visitor. I moved carefully. They could have been
little Sagrada Familias, or at long last the underwater city—
entrance beneath to petals, marvels—the fountain
of eternity! All this kept apart from the world. But no.
Like many wonders, they're found much nearer than we knew.
And I'm deflected off the pretense as off barriers
to a highway, like night-traveling trucks drifted against them,
adding another skid or strike to patterns from the others—
blue, orange, blackened pre-arcs, patches still bearing
the chalk of contact like the scraped leg of a child—
maybe from a bike spill, or from thickets, red blackberry
collecting: only later will the hurt set in. For now,
distraction. Something soars, pushing down sound—
within the camper, the higher pitch of glasses knocking
together, knocking the hutch—and out of the symphony,
giddy, an older couple emerges together from the showers,
remembering as much sharpness as years' distance
can afford, the sharp illusion of youth, and flush-warmth.

Caribou

Caribou summer coats look burnt through at the shoulder, a sound black
underrunning two pocked bodies, bite scars or molt. A cow and her bull

are slow in taking their fill from the tundra bank, mosses and brush,
polychrome, mottled, ever-shifting and more so beneath deeper

spruces back around the campground. They have been here almost daily
since I've come to visit this clear thin river.

A man and wife are there today ahead of me, shadowing the two,
and call me over to their vantage so I can see the sameness in the bodies,

what both carried—bone drawn close to contact on the bowed heads,
run parallel as a woman's parted flesh—then flown, unbraiding, in arcs.

Correction

Weeks slipping under, winter,
a plain burning into widening space—
into stubble, patches of stalks
of tall flora bloomed late, left quick,
fallen over themselves to dry.
Down to single-state.

Then I saw bright cardinal:
a male rush to hide from my chain's din,
old bike. (Red, since when?)
And two weeks later, a small company
flashing under-wing. I had no idea
of this harbor, but it is here,
it is now and has been here
and I am changed.

On Mothering

Grown diverted to light on the water
or half-felled, pine boughs with tufts soft-skirted

hang like wings, or certain petals spiriting
to three, on a bearded iris, splayed,

while three more enclose. This is what you fear—
being a soul and not able to speak.

Were we not sisters, dressed in our waders?
Were we not both dancing sisters? Mother,

when my father steadied me as I walked
sliding stones, forging the hip-deep river—

understand that fathering is a quieter endeavor.
We went forth among the red-new saplings,

the grasses, raised, that created sink-holes
in the banks—that hid small shell-spattered piles

and fish spines and soft clay—and your tumbling,
slow suffering, in the dark stiffness behind.

Morning

When the early sun hits the windows,
rows of hundreds alternating paned and free
on a factory building batter the light through,
break it, resume. Mesmerized like you,
there could be peopling there,
those who emerge at a set time and,
facing east, happen on blindness.
Is it the structure's filled entirely with morning
or that its substance has been demolished?
Is it there's violence in the dawn?
Light-filled and century-old,
ancient-industrial, it catches you
less than you are the one doing the catching.
You are the one seeing, leaving.

Confines
Valencia, Spain

The central market is contained in one structure:
weekly fair-grounds thrive inside an architectural marvel
with a dome and walls tiled in bright formations,
windows stained and shaped, though shuttered high.

Back behind the small east exit, graffitied, a family
slouches out of the sun by their bleak low-rate produce,
hand-written posters, their rowdy kids endlessly
running each other up and down the platform steps—

and the market exhausts itself after a morning,
and vendors pack and go. Emptied box stalls, fish smell,
the metal doors rolled and locked to ground seal
the building in its quiet, sending people elsewhere

through tight alleys, under a lean statue guarding
the angled and thrusting back streets as if an expansive
mausoleum, or just one red apartment—it's Mary,
or a white dog vivid against the startling sky.

The Orchard

Backing down from the dock crowned with a rotunda,
boards edge off to stone barricade to sloping beach—
more a landing than a beach—where ribbon streams cut
matte dirt into flexed sections. A small circle of grass,
sea grass, plateaus, upholds its thickness, its blades
erect but fading at the edges. Long ago the rocks
began accumulating souvenirs, cluttering their tinted clefts.

It's Sunday, the dredge won't carve out silt, in mouthfuls
gum at the underlying orchard where dispersed life blurs
with the alluvium. Groups pass on outboards,
attempt to fish, troll tube eels through the channel
writhing the black synthetic bodies with motor speed.

If one snags and breaks off, and quiets, in the dark and mire
a marvel species will emerge: ghosts, acorn worm-heads
poking in the undercurrent—descendants of hemichordata,
fusion of invertebrate and vertebrate. Branchial slits
and iodine smell, tomorrow they'll lift with the sediment,
pack into colored crates and go in barges to the sea—
then again repopulate the mouthed holes along the shore.
How long they take is anybody's guess, somewhere between
the seaweed-mimic crab in my palm and the hidden ceiling
of the rotunda, light blue, white molding forming a star.

Reckon

The tendency is for them to turn, mercurial,
heading anywhere away—white tails
to the banking hillside dappled
by new summer, by new sunlight,
everything scattering—

but then around the trail's bend
this one, decided, discomfiting face-on:
I have had lovers like him, I realize,
recognizing parts of him: one, the stance,
two, the stillness, another, the kinder
caution of his antlers, narrow-set and velvet.

I am the stiller in this encounter
and aware of being strange.
He lifts one hoof to bring it down, the other;
he is sizeable; but he is beautiful,
so I return to watch him from a ridge.
I might have shouted, but the sound
would have made something of me
I am not. I wait a small time,
and step off, and blaze along the soft forest
a semi-circle, and am gone.

Beam

Kisses the girls
hello, swooping
in a limp,
my granddad
takes twenty-five-cent
oysters Thursdays
the one bar three blocks
from his place. It doesn't
get better than that.
At a central bar table
he waxes grandiose; everyone
knows him. Trades
all the old jokes. Says
he's ready for the end. Asks
Are you married yet?
More common: states
The shop's your dad's.
He'll want a shed,
he'll want to plan.
Be surprised what you'd find
in there—this time
he added, Don't forget.
How could I,
from sheer repetition,
his obstinacy, or otherwise?—
always the tour,
Polaroids of projects,
his trophies,
file-cabinet moonshine.
Once he produced
an uneven slab—
he'd cut into it,
sanded it down, found
a remarkable burling—

like how
the wake of fine snow
drawing up after a train,
keeping time for a second,
then forgetting, suddenly,
lets what was there before,
the beamed
but traveling tracks,
be now understood more clearly
for the lapse.
He said—then waited—
What do you see?

Additional Acknowledgments

I am more grateful than I can express for the support of my poetry from my partner, Conor; my parents, Susan and Michael; my brother, Patrick; and my family and friends far and near. Particularly in the process leading to the poems in this chapbook, thank you Cate Williamson, Adam Pellegrini, and Jessamyn Smyth. My ever-enduring appreciation goes to the generosity of my poetry teachers who brought me to this writing: Alicia Ostriker, Stanley Plumly, Carl Phillips, Michael Collier, Joshua Weiner, Elizabeth Arnold, Deborah Digges, and David Rivard.

Julia Leverone has a PhD in comparative literature from Washington University in St. Louis and an MFA in poetry from the University of Maryland. She writes poems and translates poetry and prose from the Spanish.

Her poems have appeared in *Crab Orchard Review, Cimarron Review, B O D Y,* and *Sugar House Review*. Her translations of poems by the Argentine Francisco "Paco" Urondo have been published in *Witness, The Massachusetts Review, The Brooklyn Rail's InTranslation, Modern Poetry in Translation, Tupelo Quarterly, Waxwing,* and elsewhere. She is at work translating a novel by Haroldo Conti.

Julia lives in north Texas with her partner who is also a writer, Conor Burke. She is an Assistant Editor at *Asymptote* and the Editor of *Sakura Review*.

www.ingramcontent.com/pod-product-compliance
Lightning Source LLC
Chambersburg PA
CBHW060227050426
42446CB00013B/3208